IMAGES
of England

RYDE
POSTCARDS

AMŒNITAS SALUBRITAS URBANITAS

RYDE.

REG?
TRADEMARK.
HERALDIC SERIES.

IMAGES
of England

RYDE
POSTCARDS

Lynette Archer and John Woodford

TEMPUS

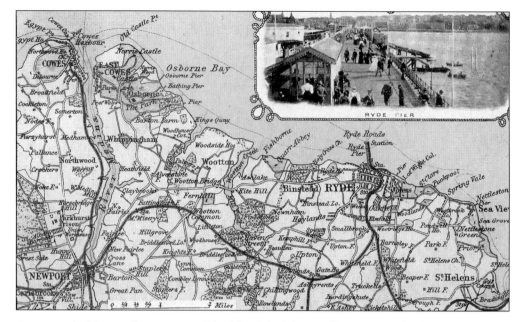

A map card of the north east coast of the Island, by John Walker & Co. Ltd. The pier is marked and also the railway. Ryde was the main gateway to the rest of the Island for the tourist trade and the transportation of goods.

Frontispiece: The Coat of Arms of Ryde. Literal translation: 'A pleasant healthy town'.

First published 2003

Tempus Publishing Limited
The Mill, Brimscombe Port,
Stroud, Gloucestershire, GL5 2QG

© Lynette Archer and John Woodford, 2003

The right of Lynette Archer and John Woodford to be identified
as the Authors of this work has been asserted in accordance with the
Copyrights, Designs and Patents Act 1988.

British Library Cataloguing in Publication Data.
A catalogue record for this book is available from the British Library.

ISBN 0 7524 2954 X

Typesetting and origination by Tempus Publishing Limited
Printed in Great Britain by Midway Colour Print, Wiltshire

Contents

A view of Ryde from the pier, dating from the 1860s.

Acknowledgements

Thanks is due to the help and encouragement of members of the Isle of Wight Picture Postcard Club; The IW County Press for information; Keith Shotter who loaned a postcard of the shop – C.W.H. Springer; Fay Brown for typing and checking an early draft.

We have, as far as possible, checked the authenticity of the material and we apologise to anyone whose copyright we may have inadvertently breached.

Introduction

The history books tell us that people were living in and around the area we call Ryde as far back as 2,000 years ago, probably around the Swanmore area, but we have to wait until the fourteenth century for further details. In 1377 the town, then called 'La Ryde', was burned down by the invading French, who also invaded Newport, Yarmouth and Newtown. After this tragic event the hamlets of Upper and Lower Ryde evolved, and by 1719, after Henry Player's son Thomas had built the first chapel, the two hamlets began to assume some size and importance.

Henry Fielding, the playwright, visited Ryde in 1753, shortly before his death, and he wrote of a major problem for people who wished to visit Ryde: 'Between the sea and the shore there was at low water an impossible gulf of deep mud, which could neither be traversed by wading or swimming, so that for one half of the twenty-four hours, Ryde was inaccessible to friend or foe'.

Eventually a jetty and pontoon partly solved the problem, allowing boats to load and unload, but in 1813 a pier was built and by 1818 the first steamboat operated services to Portsmouth, taking about thirty minutes to cross the Solent. The last years of the eighteenth century saw people of importance with money begin to build houses and invest in the area. By 1811, the first census disclosed a population of 1,601, and the early years of the nineteenth century saw great expansion. Houses and shops were built, and markets for fish, corn and cattle were established around the new Town Hall, and slowly the two hamlets grew closer together.

The pier was extended in 1827, running out across the sands some half-a-mile from the shore, making it the second longest pier in Britain. The development of the railways on the Island also helped in the growth of the area, enabling people and goods coming into Ryde to be quickly despatched to their destinations.

In 1868 the town received its charter of incorporation, with a mayor, six aldermen and eighteen councillors. Ryde also benefited from its proximity to Osborne, the residence of Queen Victoria and, for the last forty years of her life following the death of her beloved Albert in 1862, a place of virtual seclusion. The Queen was a frequent visitor to the town in these later years, coming in from Osborne by coach and attended by outriders, Queen's Road thus being named after her. Splendid public buildings were built, the most prominent being the Royal Victoria Yacht Club – whose foundation stone was laid by the Prince Consort – the Town Hall, Theatre Royal, Market House, the School of Art, the Museum and the Royal Isle of Wight Infirmary, all of which gave Ryde its distinctive Victorian appearance. By 1881, the population stood at 11,461 and though the rate of growth slowed down after that, it increased steadily and doubled to 22,500 by 1961.

The twentieth century saw Ryde established as a seaside resort and as the main port of entry for visitors to the Island, and for the decades after the Second World War the summer months saw massive crowds of people arriving for their summer holidays at resorts around the Island. In the 1960s Ryde witnessed the comings and goings of no fewer than 123 trains each day. As more and more families took to coming on holiday in their cars, those figures drastically dropped, as Ryde Pier did not have facilities for the unloading and loading of vehicles, and nearby Fishborne and Cowes benefited by this.

The following pictures of Ryde and district are a product of the excellent photographers that the town has possessed in the past. The invention of the postcard in 1894 opened a whole new industry. Locals and visitors alike could send to their friends and relatives a view of where they were living and staying for as little as one penny.

Without the efforts of Jabez Hughes, William Hogg, Frederick Broderick and others the following view of life and times of the good people of Ryde would not have been possible.

A photograph, by Hughes and Mullins of Ryde, of an early engraving that shows Ryde's library situated on a hill overlooking the Solent. Before the pier was built at Ryde, the only way to land by sea, other than beaching, was by a causeway. This is shown in the picture and is the only known view of the causeway. In the shop at the library it states there is a billiard room and a State Lottery available. The lottery was discontinued in 1823 by Parliament after determined efforts by William Wilberforce for its abolishment.

One
Early Ryde

A view of Ryde from the sea before the pier was built in 1814.

A view from the beach at Appley with the pier in the distance, 1824.

Early view of Ryde from the pier, from *Views of the Isle of Wight* by T. Nelson & Son, *c.* 1870. The engraving of Ryde Pier Head is by Rock & Co. of London, dated 1870. The horse-drawn carriages were operating by 1869.

A postcard of a Brannon engraving from an old print of 1851. The pier is in the foreground, on the extreme left is Ryde Sailing Club with a pillar frontage, and there are many hotels in Pier Street. The main difficulty in landing at Ryde was the wide mud banks, over which visitors had to be taken in a wherry as far as possible, and then carried ashore in a cart or on a man's back. This bed of mud has now been replaced by sand over which the tide recedes a long way. The pier, with additions, now replaces a length over 2,000 feet and easily overcomes these problems.

The old way of unloading cargo from boats. The boat would come in on a high tide, anchor and then wait until the tide dropped and then unload. This method of unloading, which was labour intensive and time consuming, has now ceased.

The docks were built in 1859, and filled in just twenty years later to enlarge the Esplanade.

Hotel & Esplanade Ryde.

An early letter from around the 1970s, advertising the hotels in Ryde and the splendid Esplanade.

Two
The Pier and Esplanade

This view shows a horse-drawn tramway on the pier, which was operating from 1864, with a crossover and siding, and two ticket kiosks in the foreground. The horse-drawn tramway ran from the pier head to St John's Road. It passed through an archway on the ground floor of the Esplanade holiday flats. This was situated on the corner of the Strand and Cornwall Street. The archway was filled in and replaced by a large bay window in 1927.

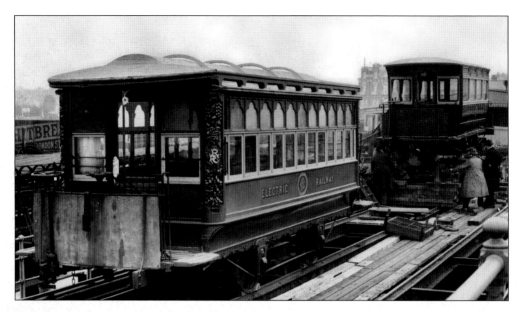

The Electric Motor Car took over from the horse-drawn tram In the foreground is the 'Grapes car', so called because of the decorations on the front. It was built at Ryde in 1868 for first class travel and originally had seats on the roof. It ran until 1927 when the line was converted to use petrol-driven trams. The tram is preserved in Hull Museum. Eventually the electric trains became more efficient and the tramway closed in 1969. It was the end of an era.

In 1927 the Southern Railway decided to replace the old trams with two petrol vehicles using the old trailer cars. This card depicts the Drewry car No. 2 arriving, which had to be jacked across the platform from the main line. They were built with Bagulay engines that were replaced with Bedford engines after the Second World War and again with diesel engines in 1959. The advertisements are for Bovril and Lifebuoy Soap – 'disinfects while cleaning'.

Diesel tram car, 1950s. Note the Brickwoods advertisement, Portsmouth Brewery. The tram is at the Esplanade station.

Merstone, 5 November 1966, drawing away from Ryde Esplanade station. In 1891, the first 'Express' train travelled from Ryde to Ventnor on 2 November in nineteen minutes, a saving of twenty-two minutes on an ordinary train. Cheap weekly tourist tickets were issued in 1892, at 10d for first class, and 7s 6d second class.

Ryde Pier and Pavilion, 1908. Coming down the pier is an early electric tram with a modified 'Starbuck' car in front and the 'Grapes' car behind. The pavilion was a splendid building and was very adaptable, able to accommodate all kinds of entertainment; in 1908 for example, roller skating was all the rage.

Ryde Pier Head, 1906, showing the departure of the *Balmoral* on a 'Round-the-Island' trip. A trip around the Island in Edwardian times cost 3s 6d.

Ryde Pier offered a grandstand view of the shipping activities in the Solent. Yachting races were organised by the Royal Victoria Yacht Club. The observation platform was always full of people with their binoculars. The yacht and the passenger steamers from Portsmouth provided endless pleasure and there was constant coming and going. The bandstand in the foreground gave many afternoon performances to the delighted audiences.

Hanging around at Ryde Pier Head, 1952 – it is not certain if this fine body of men are 'Caulkheads' or 'Grockels'. 'Caulkheads' are born Islanders and 'Grockels' are visitors that have flocked to the Island for centuries to enjoy the peace and quiet the island can provide.

Passengers disembarking from a paddle steamer at Ryde Pier in the mid-1900s. Note the ornate balustrade on the edge of the pier and the landing stage.

19   RYDE (Isle of Wight). — The King's Yacht. — LL.

Elegant Rydians gather at the Pier Head to see King Edward VII's yacht sailing by. This card was posted in August 1905.

Esplanade station showing the ticket kiosks at the entrance to the pier. Planty of shipping can be seen in the distance. Note the crane in the foreground.

An aerial view of Ryde Pier Head, showing a paddle steamer. On the right of the picture can be seen the slipway of the Vectis Rowing Club. The Esplanade station at the turn of the nineteenth century. The first pier at Ryde was built in 1813 and was 1,740 feet long. In 1824 it was lengthened to 2,040 feet and in 1827 was widened again to 2,250 feet. The Railway Pier was built in 1878-80, and was under the management of a Mr Fisher for the joint railway companies. As can be seen here, there were no buildings on the pier. The crane on the right is at the Quayside. In 1864, the Ryde to Shanklin Railway opened. It was later extended to Ventnor in 1866. In 1875, the Ryde to Newport line was opened. The Ryde to Brading line opened in 1864, and in 1882 a branch line to Bembridge opened from Brading station.

Ryde Pier from top of the 120ft pile crane, in the summer of 1931.

A view of the pier and Western Sands in 1934. The foreground shows a Punch and Judy show on the beach and a steam train on the pier. The background shows a paddle steamer at the Pier Head and an ocean liner en route from Southampton.

Miss Morant, on 18 August 1913, at Ryde Head Pier, showing the fashion of the day. 'Touting Strictly Prohibited', reads the notice. A board advertises entertainment at the Pier Pavilion.

The entrance to the pier at Ryde, photographed in Edwardian times.

A Ryde ticket collector, 1910.

Ryde Pier. The foundation stone was laid on 29 June 1813, and eventually the pier was lengthened to half a mile. In the 1860s it was widened to accommodate a pier tramway. By 1880 a railway pier was built along the side of the tramway. The end of the tram car came in the 1950s, but the railway is still in action. The line has been electrified to take the old London Underground rolling stock.

An Edwardian view of Ryde Pier, showing the landing jetties of the rowing club and swimming club. A sleek pinnace is seen leaving the area.

23

Queen Mary arriving at Ryde Pier, 1935.

Ryde Corporation purchased the Victoria Bathing Pier in 1915 for £1,000, from the Ryde Pier Company, for a development scheme. This is seen on the left of the postcard. Note the horse-drawn landaus and carriers. The cabmen's rest centre is situated in the middle of the Esplanade. Later postcards show that it was moved to the left-hand side of the road.

The entrance to the Victoria Bath Pier, also showing the railway line and tunnel under the Esplanade. This was taken before the Eastern Pavilion was built. In the distance can be seen the Canoe Lake and the pier at Appley.

Ryde had two firms operating bathing machines – Kempus and Rayners – at the turn of the century. The card shows machines belonging to B. Reeves, a firm probably established a little later.

Children watch fascinated as Punch knocks the stuffing out of Judy and vice-versa on the beach at Ryde. The Punch and Judy and Italian Marionettes Show was produced by Professor G. Day.

In 1890 Miss Brigstocke gave two drinking fountains and lamp pillars for the Esplanade.

Note the policeman making sure all is well!

The bowling green on the Esplanade at Ryde, pre-1904.

A game of bowls on Ryde Esplanade, as seen here in 1904, has changed very little over the years, except perhaps for the clothes!

Ryde's first open Bowls Tournament was held on the Corporation Green in 1919. In 1926 I.W. County Bowling Association hosted a May Tournament against the South African bowlers. The Island team won the event. The Island bowlers also defeated the New Zealand tourists in 1928.

The new pavilion in the Eastern Esplanade Gardens opened in 1927. It was acquired from the Southern Railway and took the lease of the promenade and pleasure pier.

Esplanade Gardens showing the bandstand and Dover Street.

The Canoe Lake was opened in 1880. This card was posted much later as a First World War tank can be seen in the top right-hand side of the card.

Ryde Esplanade and Canoe Lake were all built on land reclaimed from the sea. On reclamation many bodies were uncovered that had been buried at sea, bodies from the *Royal George* which sank on 29 August 1782. They were re-interred, and a small garden was planted in their memory.

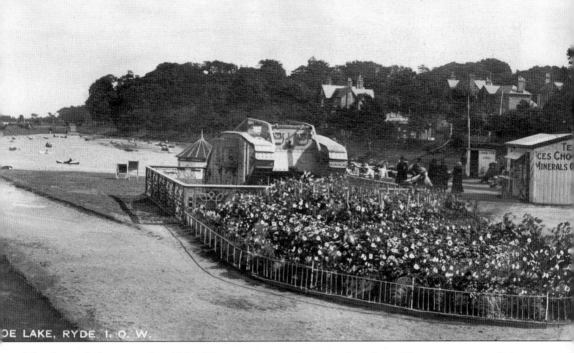

DE LAKE, RYDE, I. O. W.

The Canoe Lake opened in 1880. The water was eighteen inches deep. This picture was taken around 1925. The First World War tank in the grounds of Ryde Canoe Lake was presented to the people of Ryde in recognition of having raised £500,000 for the war effort; it was named *Louise*, after Mayoress Miss S.L. Barton.

Regattas for the young and old took place yearly, and were eagerly awaited by the spectators. This one took place in August 1920.

St Cecilia's Abbey, situated at the eastern end of the Canoe Lake. A community of Benedictine Nuns moved to Appley in 1922 from Ventnor. They took over the Abbey church and cloister, built by the community of St Cecilia's, who had lived in Ryde since 1906 before returning to France in 1922.

St Cecilia's Tower being rebuilt, c. 1906. Note the scaffolding of wood. The foreman in a Trilby hat poses with the workmen and a group of young lads. All the way up on the tower work is halted for photographs.

32

Appley Tower, showing the pier.

Appley Tower, a castellated landmark. This folly was built in about 1870 by Sir William Hutt, who then owned the Appley Estate. An alarming fire took place at Appley Towers on 22 March 1904. A splendid building with a clock tower was badly damaged. The estimate for the renovation was £3,000. It was owned by Captain G.W. Hutt.

Puckpool. During the nineteenth century, Britain regarded France as a potential enemy. The naval dockyard at Portsmouth and the three sea forts, Horse Sands, No Man's Land and Spit Bank Fort, formed a ring of defence. It was thought necessary to have additional protection, so in 1863-65 a battery was constructed at Puckpool. In 1867 the layout of emplacements were changed to accept thirty-eight mortars in two rows with five guns to cover the beach either side. In 1873 heavier guns were installed. The mortars were removed in 1888, and eleven-inch guns were installed but then removed in 1895. Between 1900 and 1901, the battery was rebuilt again. During the First World War it was mainly used as a depot for coast gunners.

After the war ended in 1918, the Battery continued to be maintained. No longer needed as a Battery, it was sold in 1928 to St Helens District Council, which opened it as a public garden in 1929. It was used again during the Second World War; ARP had a telephone centre 1939-1940. The Observer Corps had a post on top of East Mortar Magazine for plotting enemy air raids. After the 1944 D-Day invasion of France, the unit repaired damaged landing craft. After the war, the Battery once again became a garden, with a café, bowling green, tennis courts and a play area for the children. The flowerbeds are well maintained and it is possible to take a pleasant walk to the shore.

Western Esplanade, Ryde, *c.* 1904. This is a splendid view of Edwardian Ryde, taken by William Hogg, showing the bandstand with its fine dome. The imposing building (on the right) is the Royal Victoria Yacht Club, whose first stone was laid by the Prince Consort in 1846.

An advert for Sivier's Hotel in Pier Street.

*Eastern Esplanade,
Ryde, Isle of Wight.*

Royal Eagle Hotel, Pier Street. This hotel was probably built on the site of an earlier public house called The Fighting Cocks. George Beasley was the landlord in 1830. A Trade Directory in 1839 listed him as the landlord of the Eagle Tavern, Pier Street. The water fountain and early public transport can be seen in the foreground. The main façade is seen immediately behind the fountain. The building is now used as an amusement arcade; the change of use was in about 1935.

Western Esplanade, Ryde.

The council accepted £8,479 for the provision of the West Esplanade. Construction started in 1900 and Princess Beatrice opened it in 1902. Military Bands and concerts were held in the Western Gardens. Union Street can be seen on the left, as can the hotels, the bandstand, Sivier's Hotel and the Royal Victoria Yacht Clubhouse, 1910.

Three

Transport

SS *Olympic* at anchor off Ryde on 27 April 1912, twelve days after the sinking of the *Titanic*. On the morning of 20 September 1911, the *Olympic* was negotiating the exit from Southampton Water at the same time the cruiser HMS *Hawke* was coming up the Solent at speed. As the *Olympic* altered course to turn into the Spithead, the two ships were placed on a parallel course. As the *Hawke* altered course to pass astern of the liner, the suction from the *Olympic*'s wash caused the *Hawke* to ram the liner 80ft from the stern. Nobody was hurt in the collision but the two vessels were both damaged. The *Hawke* was towed to Portsmouth for repairs and the *Olympic*, after disembarking her passengers at Cowes, was taken to Southampton for inspection. The captain of the *Olympic* was E.J. Smith.

8336. S.S. "PORTSDOWN".

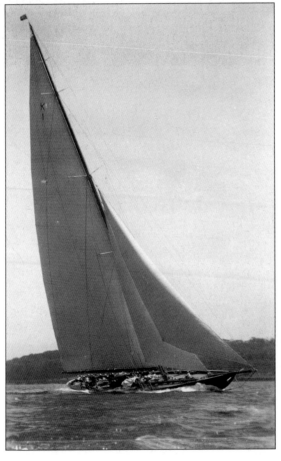

The SS *Portsdown* was built in 1928 and was a passenger paddle steamer on the Ryde to Portsmouth route. In 1939 she was requisitioned by the admiralty for war work. Helping out in the evacuation of troops from Dunkirk in 1940, the paddler crossed to France totally unarmed but, despite coming under fire from shore batteries, she returned to England with 1,500 troops. Five of the *Portsdown* crew were decorated for gallantry. After returning to normal service in the Solent, the *Portsdown* struck a mine off Spit Bank on 20 September 1941 and was so badly damaged that she sank. Twenty people were lost.

This view is from 1920, when King George V and Queen Mary paid a visit to the Yachting Festival. The King won the challenge cup in the *Britannia*.

Passengers disembarking from the *Duchess of Fife* at Ryde Pier, Whitsun, 1920.

The *Duchess of Fife*, built in 1899 by the Clydebank Engineering and Ship Building Co. Ltd, sailed between Ryde and Portsmouth. It was sold in 1929 and broken up.

South Western & Brighton Railway Companies' Steam Packet Service

—— TO AND FROM THE ——

ISLE OF WIGHT

OCTOBER 1922, and until further notice

(Weather and other circumstances permitting).

S.S. "Duchess of Fife," "Duchess of Kent," "Duchess of Norfolk," "Duchess of Albany" and "Princess Margaret."

PORTSMOUTH HARBOUR AND SOUTHSEA CLARENCE PIER TO RYDE

	WEEK DAYS														SUNDAYS				
	a.m.	a.m.	a.m.	a.m.	a.m.	a.m.	p.m.	p.m.	p.m.	p.m.	p.m.	p.m.	p.m.	p.m. (Thursdays only)	a.m. (October only)	a.m.	p.m.	p.m.	p.m.	p.m
Portsmouth Harbour dep.	2.40	7.5	7.35	9.25	10.0	11.40	12.15	1.50	3.15	3.55	4.50	6.10	7.15	11.30	10.15	12.20	2.10	4.0	6.55
Southsea Clarence Pier ,,	..	..	..	..	10.10	11.50	..	2.0	..	4.5	5.0	..	7.25	..	10.25	12.30	2.20	4.10	7.5
Ryde Pier .. arr.	3.10	7.35	8.5	9.55	10.35	12.15	12.45	2.25	3.45	4.30	5.25	6.40	7.50	12.0	10.50	12.55	2.45	4.35	7.30

RYDE TO SOUTHSEA CLARENCE PIER AND PORTSMOUTH HARBOUR

	WEEK DAYS														SUNDAYS				
	a.m.	a.m.	a.m.	a.m.	a.m.	p.m.	p.m.	p.m.	p.m.	p.m.	p.m.	p.m.	Midt. (Thursdays only)	a.m. (October only)	a.m.	p.m.	p.m.	p.m.	p.m
Ryde Pier dep.	6.45	7.55	8.40	10.10	11.10	12.55	2.20	3.5	4.0	4.50	5.45	6.50	9.25	12.5	11.10	1.10	3.10	5.0	9.25
Southsea Clarence Pier arr.	..	..	..	10.35	11.35	1.20	..	3.30	..	5.15	6.10	..	..	..	11.25	1.35	3.35	..	..
Portsmouth Harbour ,,	7.15	8.25	9.10	10.45	11.45	1.30	2.50	3.40	4.30	5.25	6.20	7.20	9.55	12.35	11.45	1.45	3.45	5.30	9.55

REVISED FARES :

	Single		Return	
	1st	2nd	1st	2nd
To Ryde Pier Gates, and vice versa. ... (Including all Pier Tolls)	2/2	1/7	4/-	3/2
To Ryde Pier Head, and vice versa. ... (Exclusive of Ryde Pier Tolls)	2/-	1/5	3/8	2/10

For particulars of

CHEAP DAY RETURN TICKETS

between Portsmouth Harbour, Southsea
Clarence Pier and Ryde
SEE SEPARATE ANNOUNCEMENTS

ORDINARY RETURN TICKETS ARE AVAILABLE FOR TWO DAYS (Including day of issue and return).

Those issued on Saturday are available to return on the following Monday. Children between three and twelve are charged half-fares.

The connection between the Trains and Boats and vice versa is not guaranteed, neither will the Joint Companies be accountable for any loss, inconvenience, or injury arising from sea risks or delays.

Passengers are requested to look to their luggage on entering and leaving the Steam Packets, and before embarking to see it labelled to the Station or Pier where the journey of the owner terminates. Passengers are allowed to take with them, free of charge, the following amounts of personal luggage: 1st Class 150 lbs., 3rd Class 100 lbs. Excess Luggage will be charged for at the rates applicable.

Goods or Merchandise not allowed as passengers' luggage, and will be charged for at Parcels Tariff.

SEASON TICKET RATES:—First Class, Twelve Months, £9 : os. od. Six Months, £5 : 5s. od. Three Months, £3 : os. od. Two Months £2 : 9s 6d. One Month. £1 : 10s. od. Available for all advertised passages between Ryde, and the Piers at Portsmouth, exclusive of Pier Tolls.

Season Tickets, exclusive of Pier Tolls, are issued at half rates for residential purposes only, to all applicants under 16 years of age, and to Scholars, Students, Apprentices, Articled Clerks and Articled Pupils (in receipt of salary, wages, or any monetary allowance whatsoever, not exceeding 18/- per week), up to 18 years of age.

Quarterly Tickets may be extended to six or twelve months on payment of the difference between the periodical rates, but tickets must be promptly renewed or the privilege will be forfeited. Application for Season Tickets should be made at the Marine Superintendent's Office, Portsmouth Harbour Pier.

CONVEYANCE OF MOTOR VEHICLES (Which can be run on and off Boats with own power), Horses, Carriages Vans, Cattle, etc., TO & FROM THE ISLE OF WIGHT on Week Days, by powerful Steam Tug and Tow Boats.

(Weather and other circumstances permitting)

From PORTSMOUTH (Broad St. Slipway) for RYDE | From RYDE (George St. Slipway) for PORTSMOUTH

About TWO HOURS before High Water. | About HALF-AN-HOUR before High Water.

Information as to actual times of departure from Portsmouth and Ryde may be obtained at the Marine Superintendent's Offices, Broad Street, Portsmouth (Tel. 4655), Portsmouth Harbour Pier (Tel. 6077), or from the Station Master, Ryde (Tel. 247).

Senders or Owners of Horses, Carriages, Motor Cars, Live Stock, etc., by Tow Boat, take upon themselves all risk of Conveyance, and of loading or unloading, as the Companies will not be answerable for accidents or damage done to any property, live stock, etc. All traffic must be at the place of embarkation half-an-hour before time of sailing, and in charge of Senders' or Owners' Servants who must accompany it.

RATES (at Owner's Risk)

		£	s.	d.
	not exceeding			
Motor Cars (See Note (A))	10 cwt., Single Journey	1	1	0
	10 cwt., Return ,, (B)	1	16	0
	above			
	10 cwt., Single ,,	1	11	0
	10 cwt., Return ,, (B)	2	16	0
Motor Tricar	..		10	0
Motor Bicycle	..		3	0
,, ,, with Side Car	..		6	0
Bicycle	..		1	0
Hand Truck or Barrow	..		2	0
Hand Organ	..		2	8
Van, not exceeding 12ft. in length (Loaded) £2 8 0	Empty	1	0	0

	£	s.	d.
Van, not exceeding 15ft. in length			
(Loaded) £3 0 0 Empty	1	4	0
,, not exceeding 18ft. in length			
(Loaded) £4 0 0 ,,	1	10	0
Farm Waggon (Loaded) £2 0 0 ,,		16	0
Four-wheel Carriage	1	12	0
,, ,, (Loaded)	2	2	0
Light 4-wheel Carriage, drawn by			
Ponies or 1 Horse	1	0	0
Gig, Cart or other 2-wheel Vehicle		16	0
Horse with Carriage		5	0
,, not with Carriage		7	0
Cattle, if under 10 in number .. each £		4	6

		£	s.	d.
Cattle, if over 10 in number .. each	4	0
When only 1 Horse or Bullock			
in the Boat ..		10	0
Yearlings .. .. each	3	0
Sheep, Lambs and Pigs—			
under half-a-score .. each	1	0
over half-a-score up to 1 score		9	0
above a single score per score	7	0
Calves .. .. each	2	6
Servants, in charge, who must			
accompany all Horses, etc. each	1	6
Dogs .. .. each	1	0
Hearse with Corpse ..	2	2	0

(A) Including Portsmouth Corporation Dues. (B) Return Tickets are available for one month.

Motor Lorries, Steam Traction Engines, Circuses, etc., Quotations by special arrangements with Marine Superintendent.

BY ORDER.

Ferry timetable for October 1922.

The Isle of Wight Express

The train seen here is heading towards St Johns station after leaving Ryde Esplanade with a fullhead of steam, on its way to Ventnor in 1920.

Ryde St Johns. *Newport* No. 25 is entering at 4.35 p.m. en route from Ryde Pier Head to Cowes. St John's station is shown on a map of 1866. The terminal buildings were extended northwards a few years later. It contained carriage and engine sheds. The sidings were extended again and a 1908 map shows locomotive, carriage and wagon works. The postcard shows engine sheds and carriage works on the right-hand side.

The waiting room of the Isle of Wight motor bus company at No. 6 Pier Street, Ryde. Pier Street was adjacent to the Esplanade from where their services started.

Thursday 13 April 1905 saw the start of the long-awaited bus service linking Ryde to many Island towns and villages. Lady Adela Cochrane, wife of the deputy governor, amid great cheering, drove the bus around the Canoe Lake and back to the Esplanade. Lady Adela can be seen at the controls and beside her are the mayor of Ryde and the company chairman.

They say 'it's quicker by rail' or 'let the train take the strain'… A railway carriage passes through Ryde on a wet day on the back of a lorry, going to Ryde St John's station.

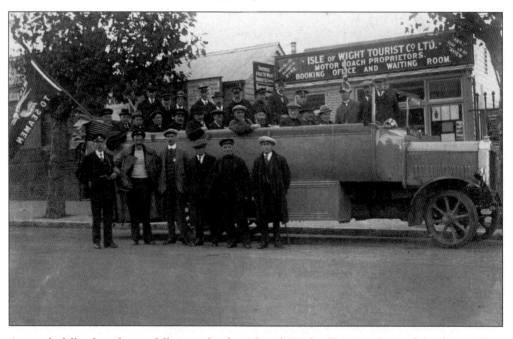

A coach-full of seafaring folk outside the Isle of Wight Tourist Co. Ltd booking office, Esplanade. The flag at the rear of the coach reads 'Mission to Seamen'. This picture was taken between 1920 and 1930.

DL77 at the top of Union Street on its way to Cowes. Originally, the syndicate proposed four different routes going out from Ryde, encompassing all the main towns. In the background is the imposing building housing the pack shops. Note the telephone lines on the building on the right.

Mr Hogg, a Ryde photographer, took this superb shot of one of the buses in front of the Pier Hotel. The local advertisement for Yelf & Co. on the front of the vehicle, goes nicely with Yelf's horse and wagon, seen on the left.

The Esplanade. The old and the new forms of transport wait for customers. Although much dearer, the buses were now the main attraction. The fare to Bembridge was 1s and to Shanklin it was 1s 2d. By rail and coach it was half these prices. The excursion coach – the Tally Ho, in the foreground – was slower perhaps, but it did not break down.

Due to the condition of the Island roads and financial difficulties, single-deck buses replaced the double-decker buses after only two years of inauguration. This postcard shows one of the new single-deckers outside of the Albany Hotel. Photographs of the single-deck buses are much rarer than are those of double-deckers.

It was announced in the *Isle of Wight County Press* in October 1905 that services would be entirely suspended until early in the following year, when single-deck buses would replace the original double-deckers. The picture shows one of the new buses making steady progress up Union Street. The bus number is DL134.

A Southern Vectis, ADL505, Dennis Lance bus waiting outside the booking office of Southern Vectis on the Esplanade. Service No. 4 went to East Cowes via Osborne. ADL505 was in service from 1936 to 1953. This vehicle was one of the first Southern Vectis double-deckers.

THE PORTSMOUTH & ISLE OF WIGHT AIR SERVICES.

The following statistics give the number of passengers carried on the Portsmouth, Southsea, and Isle of Wight Aviation, Ltd., Air Ferries: Ryde and Portsmouth—Week ended June 8 249, June 15 196, June 22 174, June 29 198, July 6 263; Portsmouth and Shoreham—9,1,0,1,6; Shoreham and Isle of Wight—4,4,3,7,4; Portsmouth and Shanklin—16,4,13,2,44; Ryde and Shanklin —18, 9, 5, 6, 11.

Statistics from the *Isle of Wight County Press* showing the number of passengers carried by the Portsmouth & Isle of Wight Air Services, 1934.

The Westland's Wessex G-ANVB, a three-engine monoplane. This aeroplane was a special version, with up to nine seats, and was built for the P.S. and I.W. Aviation Ltd, for a ferry service from Ryde to Portsmouth that began on 27 June 1932. Fares were 6/- single and 10/- return. The writer of the above postcard had travelled to Portsmouth during the afternoon of 2 August 1932 – 'it was lovely'.

De Haviland DH 82, Dragon Rapide; the *City of Birmingham* at Ryde Airport, 1938. The *City of Birmingham* G-ACPR had a pilot and radio office and could carry between five and eight passengers. The aircraft was in the service that linked the Island with all parts of the British Isles and, of course, the Continent. Passengers were picked up at Ryde and Bembridge airports.

Above: Young's horse and carriage outside the Royal Pier Hotel in 1908.

Right: Advertisement for Young's Job and Posting Establishment, dating from the 1890s.

Opposite below: D.KJ. Gipsy-engined *Moth*, 1935-1938. This aeroplane of the P.S. and I.W. Aviation Ltd was used for instruction and aerobatics. The Portsmouth, Southsea and Isle of Wight Aviation Ltd, 1939, was a private company that began operating an air route between Ryde and Portsmouth on 3 February 1934. The Ryde airport was where Tesco is now; the Conning Tower and Reception Lounge can still be recognised. The airport was not a success owing to the crosswinds. A Bembridge man, one Bill Watson, used to fly to Portsmouth to have his hair cut, clearly a case of 'one-upmanship'. As the company did not have an official contract with the G.P.O., only privately-carried souvenir mail was flown from Ryde to Portsmouth on 7 December 1934. Twelve pieces of mail were flown.

12 December 1910. The usual way of delivering heavy goods and parcels was by horse and cart. Pickford's cart can be seen in an unlocated district of Ryde.

Church Street in Swanmore. This is H. Bartlett's horse and cart, making a delivery of coal in around 1904.

Four

Hotels

An engraved billhead from the Pier Hotel, Ryde, 1870.

The Royal Pier Hotel was built in 1827 on the site of the old Passenger Hoy, which was later called the Bugle. Over the years the hotel was enlarged and it became one of Ryde's leading hotels. It was situated at the bottom of Union Street (now a large, landscaped roundabout). The premises had unrivalled sea views. The entrance in Pier Street shows the Tap Bar, with the large lantern. As it was opposite the pier entrance, horse-drawn carriages awaited passengers, the stepladder out in readiness for them to ascend to the top. As the result of an accident, when a bus overturned at the bottom of Union Street and Pier Street, the council decided to purchase the hotel and in 1927 it was demolished. This gave better clearance for vehicles to turn the corner.

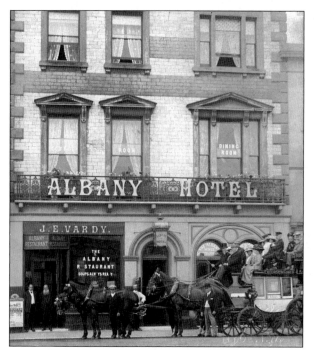

This seafront public house opened in around 1810 as the Union Tavern. It stands on the site of one of the earliest public houses in lower Ryde, called The Ship. The Ship was demolished between 1800 and 1810, and the new inn lasted until 1866. It was renamed the Union Tavern. It became the Union Vaults in 1878 and part of the adjacent Royal Eagle in 1895. This arrangement lasted until 1915, when the establishments were again separated.

York Family Hotel, George Street. This fine example of a Georgian building was demolished to make way for the Art Nouveau structure of the Royal York Hotel in 1935. The late ex-Empress Eugenie spent a night here after her escape in disguise from the Tuileries in 1870. She cam across from France in a forty-ton cutter belonging to Sir John Burgoyne and reached the hotel at about 1 a.m. accompanied by Sir John and a lady who had crossed the Channel with her.

Royal Victoria Yacht Club, built in 1846. A very imposing structure, it lies to the west of the pier, surrounded by a high stone wall. It became a public house in 1966, when the RVYC moved to its present location in Fishbourne. It was then used as a nightclub called 'Patsy's'. In 1988 the main bar closed.

The Osborne Private Hotel, as it appeared in 1906. It boasted corridors heated in winter, a pleasure garden and croquet lawn, and car for hire. Terms during the season were four guineas with Special Winter terms. The Dean House Hotel was under the same management, telephone number 88. Later it was renamed the Solent Court Hotel. A fire devastated much of the building in 1992. The façade was restored and it is now self-contained flats and apartments, with the addition of an eastern wing to the building.

Salisbury Temperance Hotel. Situated at the bottom of Union Street, the Temperance Hotel was not licensed for alcoholic drinks, and catered for people who held alcohol in abhorrence. On the left of the card was situated a shop selling alcohol! A view of the pier can be seen and there is an old gas lamp on the right.

The Royal Esplanade Hotel and Tap at No. 14 Castle Street. This is another large hotel that took the prefix 'Royal' after Queen Victoria visited Ryde in 1859. The Tap Bar in Castle Street closed in 1906. It is still a very popular hotel and is now owned by Shearings Coach holidays.

Riviera Boarding House and Yacht Clubhouse. The Riviera Boarding House is on the Western Esplanade and beyond is the Royal Victoria Yacht Club. This card is from around 1906.

"Wight Hall," Ryde, I.W.

The Wight Hall, a private hotel situated on the seafront at Ryde. Both this postcard and the following one were written in the same handwriting.

Wight Hall, Ryde, I.W.

Postcard used to advertise the Wight Hall Hotel at Ryde in 1817. The facilities included tennis and croquet. The hotel is situated on the Esplanade.

The bandstand on the Western Esplanade, on a postcard sent from Ryde on 18 August 1914. The writer notes: 'Germans have entered British East Africa, not far from Mombassa'.

The Waverley Hotel, which faced the sea and was near to the pier. The views across the Solent were magnificent. Access to sands, gardens, walks, tennis courts and bowling green were all close by. This view is from around 1920.

The Seaford Hotel was set in 'quiet and dignified surroundings'. It stood in its own grounds of two acres, which sloped to the shore, terminating in a wide terrace. It had private access to the beach on the western side of the pier, where safe bathing could be enjoyed. It was also near to Union Street and the shops and amusements, but far enough away to be secluded. All the bedrooms were fitted with hot and cold running water, box spring mattresses and gas fires. There was a ballroom and dining room (with separate tables). The exterior of the hotel faced the sea. (Ward Lock Illustrated Guide Book, 1929-30)

The Seaford Hotel advertising board can be seen here on the sea wall, intimating how close to the shore the hotel was situated. The beach, as advertised by the hotel, can be seen as a 'safe environment'. The couple on the beach are admiring the view towards the mainland.

The Dean House Private Hotel was near to the pier, with unobstructed views of the Esplanade gardens and sea, opposite bathing and boating slipways. It was near bowling greens and tennis courts.

Rear elevation of the Dean House Hotel.

The Milverton Hotel overlooked the Canoe Lake next to the putting green. It stood in its own grounds on the seafront with uninterrupted sea views. It had central heating, electric light, gas fires, box and pocket spring mattresses, table tennis and billiards. Picnic lunches were provided, and it was famed for its excellent cuisine. It claimed that foreign visitors were specially catered for. This was from around the 1920s.

Ryde Castle Hotel was a private residence until 1930. It was originally opened as a hotel, and a major extension was built to provide more space on the eastern side, which allowed extra accommodation. It was known as the Ship and Castle in the early 1960s, but in the 1980s reverted to its original name.

Westfield House was built for the second Earl Spencer. It stood on a rise with gardens sweeping down to the shore. It was an early nineteenth-century villa, with a tower similar to the one at Osborne House.

In August 1843, the house was sold to August Clifford. He employed Thomas Hellyer, a Ryde architect. He added a gallery in the 1930s, which was used as a ballroom when it became a hotel. It is now separate housing.

The Old York Family Hotel in George Street, looking towards the Esplanade and the sea. The correspondence on the back of the card reads as follows: 'Just a card of the house where I am living. It seems to be a very nice hotel. Well I suppose it was once but now, of course, it is empty bar soldiers. It is a pity that we are allowed in such places, as some do not care what they do. The rooms are very nicely decorated. I have marked with a cross the room in which I am. There are three in this room, each one being a Londoner, one from Stratford, one Shepherds Bush. Yours Arthur'. The card is dated from around 1914.

The Lion Hotel, No. 1 Garfield Road, which was originally known as The George Inn. In 1855 it became the Lion, when it was taken over by a Ryde brewer, James Lake. The pub remained open until 1973, when it was demolished and a Curry's store erected on the site.

Garfield House in Garfield Road was a Christian guesthouse for women and girls. It had accommodation for seventy visitors with a large dining hall that opened out on to a lawn and garden.

When visiting Ryde you will need Refreshments

Is it not so?

Then obtain the best from the

Gainsborough Cafe, 75 Union Street, Ryde.

Tables and Private Rooms can be booked by phone (174).

Seating accommodation for 350.

Luncheons 2/- and 2/6

Afternoon Teas from 9d.

Cecil Elgar's Orchestra
Plays during Lunch and Tea.

The Gainsborough Café was listed in the 1931-32 Hampshire and Isle of Wight Trade Directory. It was a popular venue well into the 1950s.

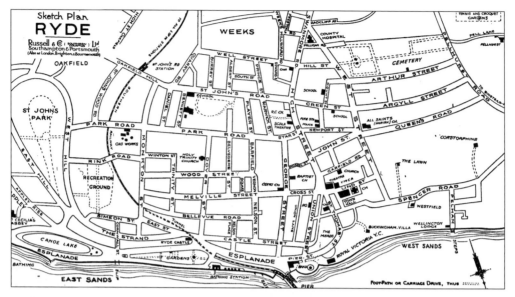

A sketch plan of Ryde in 1926, showing the general layout of the town. The Scala Theatre is now a supermarket. The County Hospital was demolished and is now a housing estate. The Theatre Royal was destroyed by fire and the remainder demolished. There is a bank on the site at present. Many changes and alterations have occurred, with a marina and entertainment centre to the left of the pier having been built on reclaimed land.

An aerial view of All Saint's church and West Street in 1924. In the left-hand corner can be seen Ryde School, a grand villa set in its own grounds. Argyle Street is in the foreground, with detached villas and gardens. John Street, opposite the church, leads to the High Street.

Five

Events

On the way to the Memorial Service for King Edward VII. Leading the way to All Saints parish church for the service is the Ryde section of the Boy Scouts, followed by a Company of the Isle of Wight Rifles. Photographed by F.N. Broderick. The shops, all shut as a mark of respect, are P. Denny and Co. (Ladies Fashions), Bevins (Clothier), still in business today, a Cycle Shop (it has a fine advert – 'Don't Trudge it – but Rudge it'). Further down the road is the Granville Hotel.

On 8 August 1837, the General Election was held. Sir Richard Simeon had been elected in 1832 for the Liberal Party with a majority of 600, but in 1835 the majority was cut to 146. He retired in favour of Captain Pelham, who was challenged by William A. Court Holmes, the Conservative candidate. The Conservatives won the seat but the result sparked severe unrest in the town, which was a staunch Liberal stronghold. The situation was aggravated by economic grievances and a local butcher, Mark Allen, was accused of charging extortionate prices and an effigy of him was burnt outside his shop. In the evening, trouble flared up outside Yelf's Hotel, the Conservative headquarters. A crowd of men assembled and marched through the town and the following morning a more serious march took place. The men carried nail-studded staves and attacked the smarter houses in Wood Street and George Street with heavy stones; the command 'Fire' was heard, followed by a pistol or gunshot. The riot was of a more serious nature than the broken windows of previous elections.

Michael Maybrick came to live in Ryde in 1892. He was destined to have a great influence on the town, having held the office of mayor five times. He was known as 'Stephen Adams' to the musical public, as the composer of *Nancy Lee*, *The Midshipmite*, *Star of Bethlehem*, *Flora*, and the *Veteran's Song*. He lived at Lynthorpe, Haylands. It was not until 1900 that he was induced to take public office. Between 1900 and 1902 many important events occurred which he presided over, notably the opening of the Western Esplanade, giving the outlet to the sea at the bottom of Union Street. He also oversaw the ceremonies in connection with the proclamation of Edward VII. His death in 1913 came as a blow to his many friends and to the public who had been acquainted with this highly respected and courteous man.

Michael Maybrick's funeral, July 1913.

The funeral procession of fireman L.A. Perkins, photographed by Hogg, 1911. Two columns of firemen march up Union Street, passing the Times Printing Works.

The funeral of Miss Brigstocke of Stonepits, Ryde. She was taken down John Street to St Thomas's church, to be interred in the family vault in November 1904. She was aged eighty years. Stonepits, in 1882, was a very old farm site, the home of the Brigstockes. Miss M.H.P. Brigstocke, a well-known benefactor of Ryde, offered to purchase the recreation ground and hand it to the town in 1900 as a free gift. This was only one of her many generous actions for the benefit of the people of Ryde. She erected and endowed almshouses and gave generous support to the County Hospital. A terrace of ten houses was built with accommodation for servants, and was named Brigstocke Terrace.

The Yeomanry returning home from camp. The Island Yeomanry and Volunteers had left for South Africa after the national call for volunteers, after a farewell inspection by Her Royal Highness Princess Henry of Battenburg. Their gallantry in the campaign has been well recorded. They are pictured here landing their horses and equipment to the west side of the pier, after returning from a summer camp in 1906.

Mr Asquith seen arriving at Ryde, en route to address Island Liberals at the Drill Hall, Newport, on 19 June 1920. Herbert Asquith was the Liberal Prime Minister from 1908 to 1916.

September 1929 saw the thrilling Schneider Trophy take place with Ryde as the centre. Over 70,000 spectators watched along the north coast of the island. The British team beat Italy in the International seaplane race over the Solent.

The winner of the Schneider Cup in 1929 was Flying Officer H.R.D. Waghorn, with an average speed of 326.63mph.

Naval Reviews were held in Spithead. This Searchlight Display and Naval Review took place on the night of 25/26 July 1924, during the reign of George V.

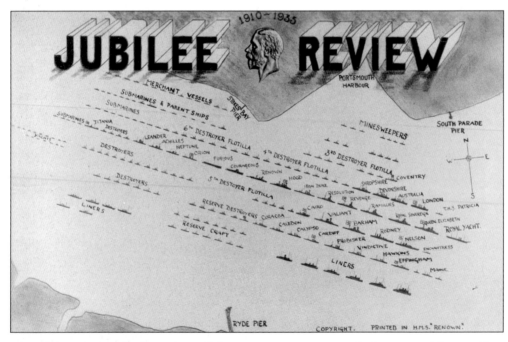

The Jubilee Review, for the Silver Jubilee events in 1935 to mark the reign of George V in Spithead.

James Conway. The photograph was taken by G. St George Biggs, No. 26 West Street, Ryde. James Conway was born in 1836 and spent thirty-five years in service in the army. Reaching the rank of Colour-Sergeant in the 91st Foot Regiment, he was awarded the three medals he is proudly wears here. They are the Meritorious Service Medal, the Indian Mutiny Medal and the Long Service Medal.

King Alfonso XIII of Spain, 1905. The King can be seen here with the cup he won at the Isle of Wight Gun Club; he was a frequent visitor to the Island, enjoying all the sporting activities that the island had to offer.

The King of Spain and Princess Ena arriving at Ryde Town Hall in April 1906, after their engagement in February. The marriage took place in Madrid on 31 May 1906. Princess Ena was the daughter of Beatrice and Henry of Battenburg.

Queen Victoria of Spain alighting from her automobile outside the shop of Mew Bros, to do some of her Christmas shopping in 1906. Mew Bros have since used this scene to advertise their business; they have this one at Ryde and others at Sandown and Southsea.

Ryde Carnival's Children's Procession on 12 September 1908. Note the elephant.

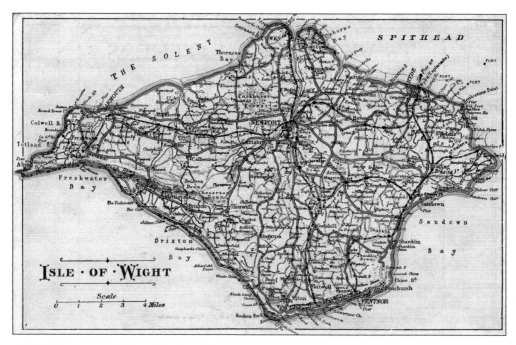

G.E. Walker's map of the Isle of Wight

A meeting of the Cycle Club at Ryde in 1911. Cycling was a very popular pastime from Victorian times onwards and there were many clubs on the Island. Ryde's club here is about to embark on a ride to meet up with another club and take tea at a suitable tea garden.

Six

Disasters

On New Years Day 1907, the *Selina*, the lifeboat at Ryde, put to sea to search for a barge skipper who had been reported missing, last seen rowing out to his vessel. It was a foul evening and the nine-man crew braved the Force 9 winds in their endeavour to find the man. They were forced to give up and turned for home. As they approached the pier, the boat was struck by a strong gust of wind and the boat capsized. The plight of the crew could not be seen from the shore and so the hours passed and the crew, clinging to the upturned boat, slowly froze. By daybreak their number was reduced to seven; Second Coxswain Henry Heward and Frank Haynes had drowned. The *Selina* was later blown ashore at Southsea, as was the man they were seeking.

WRECK of the RYDE LIFE BOAT
Crew clinging to the keel through stormy night drift to
TWO LIVES LOST
J.W.S.   Southsea

HENRY HEWARD, Second Coxswain, Perished, Jany 1st 1907.

FRANK HAYNES Coastguardsman, Perished Jan 1st 1907.

HEROES ALL!

Ryde Lifeboat Disaster, Jan. 1st, 1907.

God bless our gallant lifeboatmen !
    Who dared the stormy wave,
Risking their lives, they launch their boat,
    A stranger's life to save.

* * *

Wild was the wind, icy the blast,
    They strove with might and main,
Long was the search, Alas ! they found,
    Their search was all in vain.

* * *

Returning shorewards, on the pier
    The lights of " Home " they see,
The boat capsized ! nine gallant men
    Were struggling in the sea.

* * *

Through the long watches of the night,
    Those gallant seamen bold,
Clung to that upturned, drifting boat,
    The strong, the weaker hold.

* * *

" Father in Heaven help, and save ! "
    They cry in grief and fear,
When life and hope are wellnigh gone,
    He heard, and help was near.

* * *

For willing ears had heard their cry,
    And willing hearts, and brave,
Stretch willing hands to rescue them,
    From death beneath the wave.

* * *

But two brave hearts had ceased to beat,
    Before they reached the shore,
Two cheery voices, silenced now,
    Silent for evermore.

* * *

Then let this cry, ascend on high,
    From people great and small,
God bless our gallant lifeboatmen,
    God bless them ! Heroes all !

M. A. SPENCER

Albert REEVES.
A. LINNINGTON, Jun.
DAN. REEVES.
A. LINNINGTON, Sen.
Jan 1st 1907
W. BARTLETT.
Ernest COTTON.
Geo. JEFFREYS.
SURVIVORS :
SELINA.

A card commemorating the sad disaster to befall Ryde lifeboat, the *Selina*, in January 1907.

'In Memoriam' postcard by F.A.N. Broderick to the crew of the *Selina*. The poem is by M.A. Spencer. The Mayor of Ryde, Mr A.J. Coombes, initiated a relief fund for the men's families. Princess Henry of Battenburg, as patron of the I.W. Lifeboat Board, sent her sympathies and a generous contribution to the fund.

Above and below: The funeral procession for the Ryde lifeboat disaster victims – Second Coxswain Henry Heward and Frank Haynes.

Ashley Gardens are a tribute to the men who lost their lives in 1907. The garden also contains a monument to a disaster from an earlier date:

> In Memory of the many officers and men of the Royal Navy and Marines who lost their lives when the *King George* sank at Spithead on 29th August 1782, and who lie buried along this seafront. And here by friends unknown, unmarked, unwept they rest.

This memorial was unveiled by Earl Mountbatten of Burma, on 31 August 1965.

Appley Park, *c.* 1908. A tree has fallen in a gale. The gardeners, who are clearing up the debris, stop awhile and pose for the camera.

The flooding of the railway tunnel, due to heavy rain in October 1909. The tunnel is below high tide level and therefore prone to flooding.

The Great Engine at work on the flooded tunnel, Ryde, 28 October 1909. Fire engines from other towns were called to help with this emergency, and it took several days to restore normal working of the trains to various parts of the Island.

Damage done to the sea wall, east of Ryde, by the high tides in December 1905. Repairs were being carried out to rectify the extensive damage.

Extensive damage was caused by a severe gale on the night of 4/5 November 1916. Note the erosion and position of the shelter.

In October 1909, abnormally heavy rains transformed valleys into lakes and caused considerable damage by flooding. The Simeon Arms, opened in 1869 by Gales of Horndean, was a free house in the mid-1880s. The lands around were named after the Simeon family. C. Read, job master, lived in the building next door to the Simeon Arms.

Drier conditions prevail at the recreation ground, 1910. The boys are playing ball. Note the cycle. All Saints church can be seen in the background.

The skating rink opened in 1910. This is it pictured after the gale on 12 September 1921.

Printed on the back of this card, 'Admiral Jellicoe's Tribute to the Isle of Wight' attempts to dispel statements alleging that the island was not safe to visit by claiming it to be the 'Safest Place in the World', because of the Zeppelins flying over London. Originally printed in the *Daily Chronicle*, 9 March 1915.

Seven
Shops and Services

The plaque on the wall reads: 'Quelch's Private Stables, Stalls and Coach Horses. To let by the week, month or year. Furniture Stores, Office 93 Monkton Street, Ryde'. Many of Ryde's wealthier residents would hire a carriage, thus saving the expense of keeping their own. The livery stables were very much in demand. The scene is at Winton Street Stables.

Ryde and east Cowes decided to follow the example of Sandown and Shanklin by obtaining a steam fire engine. The first steam engine was purchased in 1908 and manufactured by Merryweather & Son.

Oakfield Post Office, 1905. Alfred Adames Tutte was the postmaster at this time, the office being a rural sub-office to Ryde. The shop was also a grocers and bakers. Staff and villagers pose outside the shop, which is situated on the corner of Oakfield Hill and St John's Wood Road; also at the scene is the village policeman. This is a splendid photograph by an unknown photographer. Does anyone know what the box on the left was used for?

Oakfield Post Office, *c*. 1895. This is an earlier photograph than the previous item (note the ivy just beginning to show). It depicts the firm's bakers, shop assistants and, of course, the postman.

George Street Post Office, Ryde, 1908. The sub-postmaster at the post office was William Robert Hogg, the photographer. He combined the running of the office with his photography. In the doorway a sign reads, 'Photographic Dark Room for Amateur's Use'. A fine selection of his postcards can be seen in the shop window, along with crested china, buckets and spades, and 'Shag' tobacco at 4d per ounce. As old age approached, the running of the office was taken over by his daughter, Mrs Reid, (possibly visible here in the doorway). Mr Hogg died in 1928, aged eighty-four.

Here is the Fish Shop at No. 1 George Street in 1962, with Mr Arthur Williams Tims (known as Bob). The poster shows a wrestling match between Rebel Ray Hunter and Judo Al Hayes at the Town Hall, Ryde, on Friday 14 July 1962 at 8 p.m. Prices 12s 6d, 10s 6d and 5s. The poster on the door reads: Crabs and Lobsters 2s, Jellied Eels 2s 3d, Cockles 9d, Whelks 1s, Mussels 1s, Oysters, Prawns, Shrimps, Dressed Crab, Crab Sandwiches, Minerals etc.

A barrel organ outside the cycle shop of R. Battersby & Son at Ryde. The event is a 'Self Denial Week', sponsored by the Salvation Army. A 'bobby' keeps an eye on the crowd. The window at the right has a fine selection of oil lamps for the cycles on show. The Battersby family still run the shop to this day.

VICTORIA COFFEE TAVERN,
36, HIGH STREET, RYDE, I.W.
Five Minutes' walk from the Pier or Railway.

Good Accommodation for Commercial Gentlemen and Excursionists.

HOT JOINTS DAILY FROM 12 to 3.

Dinners with Vegetables, 9d and 1s each.
Breakfasts and Teas from 6d.
GOOD BEDS, 1/- AND 2/- PER NIGHT.

SCHOOLS AND DINNER PARTIES CONTRACTED FOR.
CHARGES STRICTLY MODERATE.

H. JAMES, PROPRIETOR.

Advertisement for the Victoria Coffee Tavern.

Pier Street, Ryde. Harvey's Café can be seen in the foreground on the left-hand side. Further along on the same side can be seen Barratt's Isle of Wight Rock Shop, which was still in existence in the 1950s. Pier Street disappeared when the Pier Hotel was demolished in the 1930s.

A street scene, showing the Roman Catholic church. It is a view of the High Street, and Turner and Sons, drapers and distempers shop, can be seen in the foreground on the left-hand side. This is of around the 1930s.

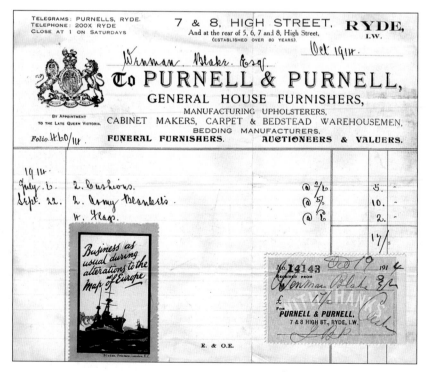

An invoice of Purnell & Purnell. Note the 'Business as Usual' sticker.

A view of the High Street, showing La Nouveaute gift shop and G.E. Mear's bakery. Note the pony and trap and the Edwardian fashions. It is around 1905.

The Prince of Wales public house is pictured here in the foreground, on the left-hand side, in around 1910. It closed down in the 1930s.

The Eagle Hotel dominated this part of the High Street with its statue of an eagle (it is still there). Next door is the post office and then Pink's, the grocers. The car number is DL9490.

SCALA
RYDE
6.15 Twice Nightly 8.40

Thurs., Fri., Sat., Aug. 14th, 15th, 16th
Matinees Wet Days and Saturday at 2·30
All Talking

PAINTED FACES
FEATURING
JOE E. BROWN.

A tensely dramatic story of a clown's love and vengeance, played against big circus backgrounds and in the jury room of a Criminal Court.

Mon., Tues., Wed. Aug. 18th, 19th, 20th
All Talking
A SENSATIONAL DRAMA!
ANN HARDING
IN

HER PRIVATE AFFAIR

In a moment of youthful indiscretion, she put herself into the hands of a scoundrel, who swore love for her and sought to win her ! To save her husband's name, she paid the price—then . . .
An unforgettable epic of the screen—abrim with thrills and tension.

Thursday Next: **UNDERTOW.**

A 1930s advertisement for the Scala cinema.

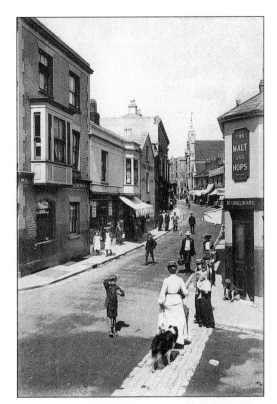

The Malt and Hops, situated at the junction of St Johns Road and Green Street. It was known as the Oak until 1872. It closed in 1928 and was then demolished, and public conveniences built on the site. These in turn were pulled down and more modern facilities erected. There is a cobbled crossing for the ladies to cross, to avoid soiling their long dresses on the mire of the highway.

Very little of Ryde High Street has changed over the years since this postcard from the 1920s was printed. However, the Manor Auction Rooms and Stores have gone completely and Lloyds Bank's new building is now there. A few of the old Ryde names can be seen over the shops – H. Pack and Co., Duffet's, B. Chapman (stationer) and Hallett's (grocer).

T. Dimmer & Son, booksellers and stationery shop, in the High Street. This shop is entered in the 1931/32 Trade Directory for the town. Note all the postcards for sale and letter cards! They also sold Bibles, prayer and hymn books, purses, handbags, manicure sets, ebony and tortoiseshell, hall sets, stationery, and initials were stamped for free, according to the long board on the right of the doorway.

C.W.H. Springer, grocers, No. 36 Swanmore Road, Ryde. This business was recorded as operating in a 1930/31 Trade Directory, loaned by K. Shotter.

Union Street from the shore, 1908. Union Street and part of the Esplanade were completed in 1856. In 1899 a bill was passed, confirming the provisional order for Ryde Corporation to purchase certain properties, to open up Union Street to the sea at what is now the Western Esplanade, after meeting opposition by the Pier Company.

The Esplanade bazaar shop on the corner of the Esplande and George Street. The shop was very popular with visitors who puchased souvenirs and gifts.

This imposing building, which contained S. Pack & Co., Drapers and Outfitters, was photographed on 24 March 1906. This business traded in St Thomas Square until the 1960s. The water trough and lamps have since been removed. There are telegraph poles over the post office in Union Street, and Timothy White's shop is on the corner with the white lighting lamps.

By the 1780s Union Street had been planned and laid out, thus linking Lower Ryde – the fishing village – to Upper Ryde. Electricity for public use was switched on by the mayor, Mr A. Millward, at the local works of the I.W. Electric Light Company on 1 October 1903.

Cross Street seen from its junction with George Street. Wilson's chemists shop can be seen on the left-hand side in the foreground. The shop is still in use as a chemist to this very day.

The Royal Victoria Arcade was opened in 1836 and was saved from demolition in the early 1970s. The tall building next to the Arcade was Jabez Hughes' photographic studio.

Cottages were demolished to build Lind Street. In 1824 the Town Hall was built. The original Town Hall was extended in 1868. It has a very classical frontage, supporting a clock tower and built to carry a clock, which was presented by the Brigstocke family. An assembly room with rounded windows was added at the same time. James Sanderson built the colonnaded building, just visible, in 1835. The Turks Head opened around 1850 and was originally known as the Yorkshire Inn. It was one of Edward Sweetman's pubs. It had the unusual distinction of having no customer toilets. The public conveniences in the Town Hall were used. It closed in 1972.

RYDE AND DISTRICT BAND OF HOPE UNION, TOWN HALL, MARCH 22 1908.

This fine organ was erected as the town's memorial of Queen Victoria's Diamond Jubilee, and was officially unveiled in July 1898. The picture shows Ryde and District Band of Hope Union on 22 March 1908.

The Royal Isle of Wight County Hospital was built in 1848 and opened on 9 November 1849, the date chosen to coincide with the birthday of the Prince of Wales. There were twenty-five beds. Prior to the opening of the hospital, patients had to travel to Winchester, which was a difficult and expensive journey. Over the years, the hospital was considerably enlarged due to the generosity of the island people and other, mostly royal, benefactors. There were no special places reserved for casualties until the turn of the century. They would be transported by the hospital's own horse ambulance, a service for which the hospital charged two guineas! Princess Beatrice opened new buildings for an out-patients ward in July 1907. Queen Victoria had previously opened the children's ward on Friday 19 July 1899. Princess Beatrice unveiled a bust of Queen Victoria, under an inscription: 'Built and endowed as the Isle of Wight's commemoration of Queen Victoria's Diamond Jubilee. She brought her people lasting good.' The bust now resides in the foyer of St Mary's Hospital, Newport, salvaged when the hospital was sadly demolished in 1996.

A group of hospital staff but with the addition of Matron, sisters and nurses. The gentleman was the chairman of the hospital committee.

Staff at the Royal Isle of Wight County Hospital at the turn of the century, posing on the steps of Victoria, the children's ward.

The 'Beggar Nelson'; the dog collected money for the Isle of Wight Infirmary. The word 'infirmary' was dropped in 1906 from the hospital's title. The dog also advertises the 'Old Curio Shop' in Ryde.

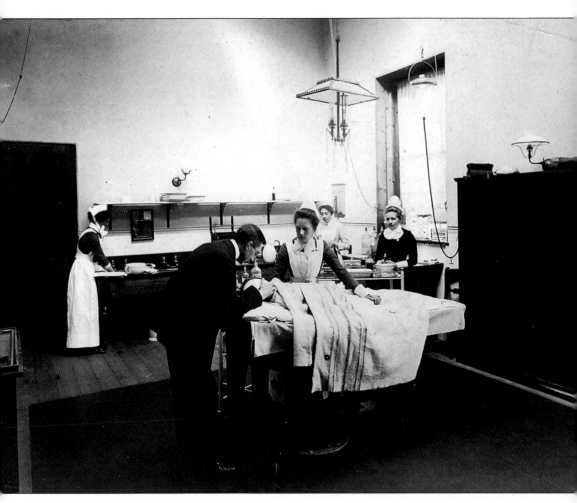

The casualty department of the Royal Isle of Wight County Hospital, c. 1880.

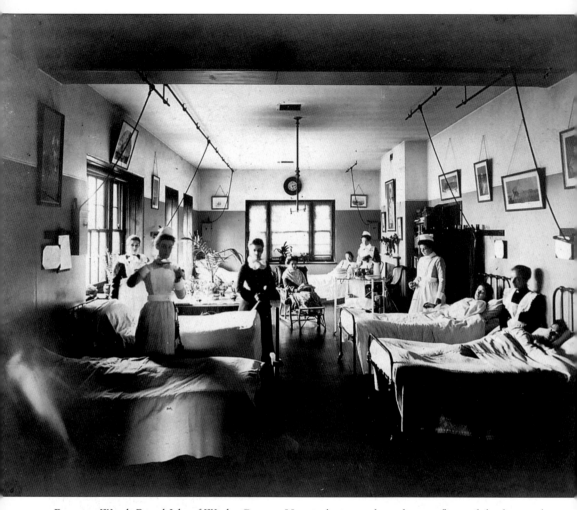

Beatrice Ward, Royal Isle of Wight County Hospital, situated on the top floor of the hospital. This view is from the 1880s.

The remains of Cottle and Calthorpe wards on the left. The front door is intact. This photograph was taken on 3 July 1996.

A view of Partlands Avenue, photographed by Matthews & Son at the beginning of the century, and there was not a house to be seen.

High Park school situated in Salisbury Road, Ryde. This was a school for girls only.

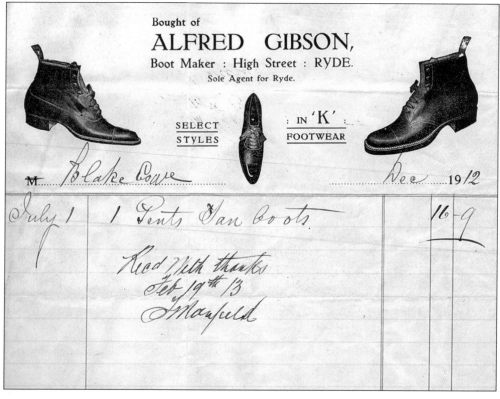

Invoice of Alfred Gibson, whose shop was in the High Street, 1912.

Eight
Churches

All Saints church in Queens Road was designed by George Gilbert Scott and completed in 1872. The Jubilee was celebrated in January 1922. Princess Christian laid the corner stone in 1869. The parish church was constituted in 1866, during the vicariate of Canon Alexander Poole. Prior to that it formed part of Newchurch parish. The first vicar, Revd W.H. Girdlestone, officiated in a temporary iron church. The spire can be seen clearly from Portsmouth and is a danger to low flying aircraft. It rises to 180ft. There is seating accommodation for 1,300 people.

St Thomas's church, St Thomas's Street, was built in 1827 on the site of a small chapel. This chapel was built in 1719 by Thomas Player Esq., Lord of the Manor. As Ryde's population grew the chapel proved too small, so George Player had St Thomas's church erected at a cost of £3,500. Today, sadly, it is not a church; the building still stands but without a steeple. This card was published by W.R. Hogg, No. 2 George Street, Ryde.

Below: The Theatre Royal stood on St Thomas's Square. It was the most historic theatre in the South of England. It was built in 1871 on the site of an older theatre and was capable of holding nearly 1,000 people, and had a very ornate interior. It was burnt down on Monday 19 May 1961, and only the front entrance survived. The interior walls were left weakened and it had to be demolished, and by the end of the week was a pile of rubble. A bank now stands on the site.

St. Thomas's Church.   Ryde I. o. W.

68   RYDE (Isle of Wight). — Wesleyan Chapel. — LL.

The Wesleyan chapel in Garfield Road is now the Methodist church. On the right of the church is the hall, giving internal access to the church.

35 RYDE (Isle of Wight). — St-James Church and Town Hall. — LL

St James' church in Lind Street was erected in 1827 by Alderman William Hughes of London, who later sold the church to Revd Waldo Sibthorpe, one of the first incumbents. It has seating for 1,120 people and of these seats only around 360 were free, because in those far-off times the minister's income was solely derived from seat rents.

105

St Michael and All Angels, Swanmore, was designed by the Revd William Guy. The foundation stone was laid in 1861 and the church opened in April 1862. It was consecrated in August 1863 and an organ was installed in 1880.

St Mary's Catholic church in the High Street, dedicated to the Immaculate Heart of Mary. It was built in 1846 with the house and school, the benefactor being Elizabeth, Dowager Countess of Clare. It was opened in 1849. The Lady chapel was added in 1893.

St John's church was built to the designs of Ryde architect Thomas Hellyer. It stands at the top of East Hill Road. Building began in 1843. Note the pram and the smartly dressed driver of the landau.

Holy Trinity church, Dover Street. The church was consecrated in 1845 and was designed by Thomas Hellyer. Mrs Lind laid the foundation stone in October 1841. There is seating in the church for 1,100. In 1845 the parish assigned to it was formally part of the parish of Newchurch.

The first Congregational chapel was built in 1802 in George Street.

This card shows the third church to be built on the site. It was erected in 1870 and demolished in 1974.

Nine

Entertainment

A Ryde Salvation Army Band, from a postcard posted on 7 May 1923.

Tenth Island Rover Moot at St Clare, September 1956. The house has since been demolished.

THERE WAS A YOUNG LADY OF RYDE
WHO ATE STOLEN GREEN APPLES AND DIED
THE APPLES FERMENTED, INSIDE THE LAMENTED
AND MADE CYDER, INSIDE HER, INSIDE.

Left: At the Theatre Royal, Ryde, on 13 March 1913. This is Consul, who rode a cycle on the stage at the Rink Theatre at Newport and at Ryde. He later dismantled the cycle and continued his act riding on the front wheel only. *Right*: A limerick of Ryde, found in Wannock Gardens, Polegate, Sussex.

The Roller Skating Carnival at the Pier Pavilion, 30 January 1908.

A 'pull-out card' containing a strip of views of Ryde.

"Having fun with
The Ryde Buccaneers"

Postcard issued to promote the activities of the Ryde Buccaneers, who were good at relieving people of their money... for charity. This card is from around 1950.

Here's One for You from
RYDE, I.O.W.

This pull-out card contains multiple views of Ryde. This type of postcard was popular among visitors who wanted to show friends and relatives Ryde's amenities.

Ten

Suburbs

The Battery Hotel, Springvale; this was described as a most comfortable and inexpensive establishment. It is situated directly on the sea front, with a panoramic view of Spithead. It had lovely tea gardens and these can be seen at the side of the building, where the two ladies are standing with the parrot in the cage. E.A. Faulkner was the proprietor. The billboards depict many firms in Ryde – Purnell & Purnell, selling furniture, carpets, bedsteads; W. Teague, pianos and organs; Wallis Riddett and Co. advertising the Freehold of Appley House and other residences in Ryde; and Messrs Coombes of Cross Street, auctioneers and valuers of furniture.

Springvale is a small hamlet between Seaview and Ryde. The houses here have a fine view of Spithead and the mainland. In earlier centuries the flat ground between Springvale and Seaview were used to make salt. This photograph is from around 1920.

66   SPRING VALE (Isle of Wight). — Near Ryde. — LL.

A view of Spring Vale from the sea wall, adjacent to Puckpool Battery. The boat has been beached so that the guns at the Battery can be shipped away. A gun can be seen on the first raft ready for the high tide, then the raft would float and the ship's crew would bring the raft alongside ready for lifting on to the ship. This postcard was sent from Seaview in February 1910.

114

Ashey Racecourse, near Ryde, in 1906. This is a very rare postcard by an unknown photographer.

The Ashey Racecourse opened in 1882 for flat and hurdle racing, and for steeple chasing. The purchase enclosure and development by a syndicate of the Ashey Racecourse as a sporting centre was decided upon, and Captain H.C. Bertram was appointed Secretary of the Races.

Outside the post office in Upton Road, Haylands, 20 July 1906. The post office was in existence from 1888 and also sold groceries. Everyone in the road is posing for the photograph! A delivery boy stands with the breadbasket over his shoulder and the women show their babies proudly.

Haylands Sunday school Band of Hope, 1907.

Sherwood Nursing Home, the front elevation. The house is now a private residence.

A child with a besom stands in the well-tended gardens at the rear of Sherwood House.

Stephen Salter designed this group of houses in Nettlestone. They are all named after universities, for example Oxford and Cambridge.

The Lodge to the Woodlands Vale Estate, built in 1900.

Stephen Salter's house, Pondwell. He was an architect.

A recently-built house on the main road to Ryde. The village of Nettlestone grew around the Village Green. The Green is still in it's original location today. This photograph was taken by F.N. Broderick of Ryde in 1909.

Nettlestone, 27 September 1930. This is a view of the village of Nettleton, a few miles from Ryde. The picture show the main road to Ryde. The village public house, The Roadside, can be seen on the right. The village developed in the early nineteenth century as a salt works, and on early maps appears as Nettleston, Saltern. The village has a Village Green.

Children in Binstead. The local school was built in 1853 for 146 children. The site was given by Mr J. Fleming, Lord of the Manor, in 1906. The village public house is named the Fleming Arms after the gentleman.

Empire Day at Binstead school, 1909.

Binstead Hill is on the main road from Ryde to Newport. Notice that there are no buildings on the left, although the school is visible on the left-hand side at the bottom of the hill. The houses on the right remain much the same today.

Hazelwood, which stood in Ashey Road, was a YMCA holiday home for young businessmen. The building was of a resplendent style, with a central tower and spire. It stood in its own grounds, which were well kept and had walks around the gardens. It overlooked the railway near St John's station. A new wing was added during the early 1900s. A post box was situated in the wall outside and many postcards were written from Hazelwood to relatives and friends, all saying how much they were enjoying their stay. In 1943, during the Second World War, a bomb exploded in the grounds in front of Hazelwood, killing four soldiers who were billeted there. The building was wrecked. Today Swanmore County Middle School stands on the site.

Office belonging to the secretary of the Hazelwood. Note the marble clock on the mantelpiece and coal fire.

Ryde Minstrel Society at Hazelwood. This was their Christmas entertainment on 22 December 1916.

At the crossroads at Havenstreet in 1926 – showing the monument on the hill to the memory of 2nd Lieutenant Richard Willis-Fleming, who was killed in action at the battle of Romani in the First World War. The monument also serves as a memorial to the men of the village of Havenstreet who gave their lives in the First World War.

Havenstreet is one of three places that suggest the possible existence of Roman roads (the other two being Rew Street, near Cowes, and Street Place, near Calbourne). The Roman roads would be hard to locate, as ground levels rise over the years and could be, now, several feet below the present surface levels. The road runs past a farm and then descends into the village, this being the main road from Ryde to Newport. Traffic jams often occur on this narrow road. It is served by buses, which adds to the complications of farm and holiday traffic negotiating the narrow part of the village.

The entrance to Longford House, Havenstreet, c. 1907. Built in the 1850s as a vicarage, the house was enlarged by a Mr Ryland, who purchased the property in 1882 and renamed the house Longford.

The Lawn, Longford House, Haven Street, I.W.

Longford House as seen from the extensive gardens of the house. From the tower there is a splendid view of the surrounding countryside. The house does not show any sign of the foliage that covered the house in later photographs. This view is from around 1907.

LONGFORD HOUSE, HAVENSTREET ISLE OF WIGHT.

Longford House in around 1912, five years on from the previous picture; the foliage now covers the whole house and a tennis court has been built on part of the lawn.

Above: One of the many sitting rooms at Longford. The only item missing from this Edwardian period room is the potted aspidistra, but there are daffodils on a table.

Above left: Mr and Mrs Ryland pose for the photographer in front of Longford House. The Rylands – Mr Ryland was a wealthy merchant from Manchester – used the house as a summer retreat, entertaining their family, friends and neighbours.

This postcard is addressed to Mr Bullock, Hill Side, Havenstreet, who was a coachman to Mr and Mrs Ryland. The picture shows Mr Bullock at Longford House with his passengers. Posted September 1908.

The road to the church at Havenstreet, *c.* 1910. Granny watches over the children who are happily playing in the road on a summer afternoon.

The church at Havenstreet, dedicated to St Peter, was built in 1852 to serve the parish formed from Arreton and Newchurch. This view is from around 1910.

Approaching the village of Havenstreet from the south. The picture shows part of the railway station.

The White Hart Inn owes its name to Richard II, whose coat of arms included a white hart (an albino red deer). The Inn is still a very popular venue and a pleasant place to end the book.